Science Technology Engineering Math

STEM STARTERS FOR KIDS

GEOLOGY
ACTIVITY
Book

PACKED WITH ACTIVITIES AND GEOLOGY FACTS

Written by Jenny Jacoby

Designed and illustrated by Vicky Barker

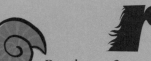

Racehorse for Young Readers

Racehorse for Young Readers books may be purchased in bulk at special discounts for sales promotions, corporate gifts, fund-raising or education purposes. Special editions can also be created to specifications. For details, contact the Special Sales Department at Skyhorse Publishing, 307 West 36th Street, 11th Floor, New York, NY 10018 or info@skyhorsepublishing.com.

Racehorse for Young Readers is a pending trademark of Skyhorse Publishing, Inc.®, a Delaware corporation.

Visit our website at skyhorsepublishing.com

10 9 8 7 6 5 4 3 2 1

Production by Madeleine Ehm

Printed in China

Copyright © 2019 by b small publishing ltd.

First Racehorse Publishing Edition 2019

ISBN 978-1-63158-427-5

WHAT IS GEOLOGY?

Geology is the study of what makes up our planet, Earth; our natural landscape; and what is deep below us. That includes the rocks, how they came to be there, why they are the way they are, and the ways they change over time.

WHAT IS STEM?

STEM stands for "science, technology, engineering, and mathematics." These four areas are closely linked, and each of them is used in geology. By studying the Earth, scientists and engineers can use technology to make our lives better, by the way we work with the natural landscape. That could be finding the best place to build a bridge, or working out how to protect ourselves against earthquakes.

Science

Technology

Engineering

Math

GEOLOGICAL TIME

Planet Earth is older than it's possible to imagine—**4.543 billion years old.**
In that time, rocks have been forming and re-forming over and over. But all this
happens very slowly—in our own lifetime, the Earth hardly seems to change at all.

It is rocks that tell us the story of Earth's history. Because rocks change so
slowly they can tell us how Earth used to look over long periods of "rock time"
(known as "geological time") long before humans were around. And one of the
stories the rocks tell is that Earth has looked very different in the past.

Once, 335 million years ago, all of the
land on Earth was in one huge piece, a
supercontinent called Pangaea. Then,
175 million years ago, Pangaea slowly
began to break up into pieces.
Those pieces formed the continents
we know today.

Antarctica

Australia

North
America

Africa

South
America

Eurasia

Can you spot today's continents within Pangaea? Color them in the matching colors. Some are tricky!

Pangaea is not the only supercontinent that has been on Earth but it is the most recent one. Other supercontinents that came and went before Pangaea include Nuna, Rodinia, and Gondwanaland. What name would you give a supercontinent?

_____

_____

VOLCANOES

Most of our planet is extremely hot, like a ball of fire. It's so hot that rocks melt. It is just the top layer, the crust, that makes up the things we recognize: the land and sea.

In some places the molten rock from the mantle rises up and bursts through the crust. This is a volcano. Some parts of the world, such as Indonesia and Iceland, have a lot of volcanoes.

CRUST

MANTLE

OUTER CORE

INNER CORE

Did you know?
Volcanoes don't keep erupting forever.
Eventually they die out and become perfectly
safe mountains.

MANTLE

ROCK FACTORY

Planet Earth is one giant rock factory. Rocks are made very slowly but every minute of every day they are being made, broken, and re-made.

There are three types of rock, and they're all made differently.

Igneous rocks
are rocks that were once melted —perhaps as volcano lava—and then cooled down. Different rocks are made depending on how quickly the lava cools down and turns to rock.

Sedimentary rocks
are made very slowly by layers and layers of earth forming on top of each other. Over time, pressure from the layers above turns them to rock.

Metamorphic rocks
have been through changes—they may have started out as igneous or sedimentary, but changed type by getting very hot or buried under a lot of pressure.

MAGMA

Can you find these rocky words in this wordsearch?

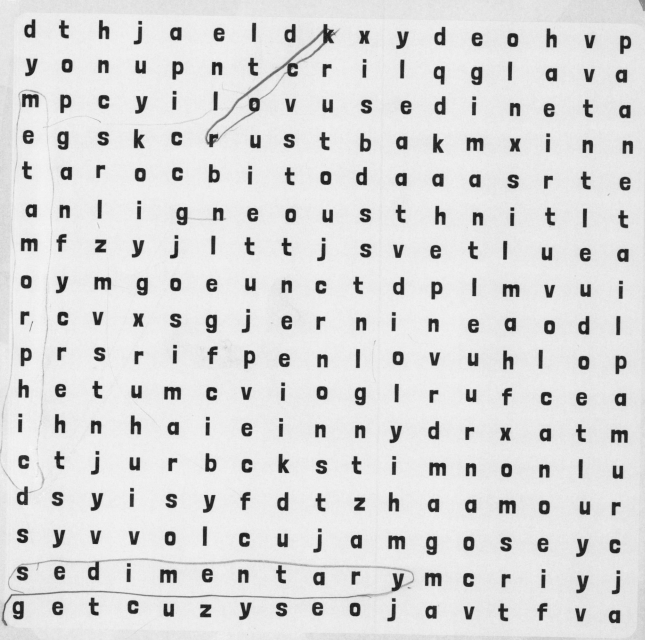

d t h j a e l d k x y d e o h v p
y o n u p n t c r i l q g l a v a
m p c y i l o v u s e d i n e t a
e g s k c r u s t b a k m x i n n
t a r o c b i t o d a a a s r t e
a n l i g n e o u s t h n i t l t
m f z y j l t t j s v e t l u e a
o y m g o e u n c t d p l m v u i
r c v x s g j e r n i n e a o d l
p r s r i f p e n l o v u h l o p
h e t u m c v i o g l r u f c e a
i h n h a i e i n n y d r x a t m
c t j u r b c k s t i m n o n l u
d s y i s y f d t z h a a m o u r
s y v v o l c u j a m g o s e y c
s e d i m e n t a r y m c r i y j
g e t c u z y s e o j a v t f v a

igneous   volcano   river
metamorphic   magma   lava
sedimentary   mantle
rock   crust

Answers on page 30.

9

EARTHQUAKES

The land and sea of the Earth's crust are all sitting on huge rocky "plates." Points where the plates meet can be fragile, and the plates are pushed apart in some places and crash together in others. Usually the plates rub together so gently you don't notice it, but sometimes the rubbing causes earthquakes that we do notice.

The central point of the earthquake, where the quake is usually strongest, is called the **epicenter.**

RICHTER SCALE

SCORE	EFFECT
1	Too weak to be noticed by people
2	Some people might notice wobbles, but no damage done to buildings
3	Can be noticed by people, lamps and pictures may swing—but no damage
4	Most people will notice objects rattling or falling off shelves—but no damage
5	Everyone would notice the shaking and some buildings might be damaged
6	Violent shaking in the epicenter can be felt for hundreds of miles
7	Most buildings will be damaged and some completely destroyed
8	Even earthquake-resistant buildings will be damaged
9	Nearly total destruction and the ground permanently changed

HAITI

ENGLAND

ITALY

Can you grade these earthquakes using the Richter scale?

Draw scenes of what these earthquakes might look like...

CHILE

SOUTH ISLAND OF NEW ZEALAND

JAPAN

3 People sitting in their homes noticed the pictures on their walls started swinging.

6 The cathedral half collapsed, and a big bend appeared in the railway line.

8 All the buildings were destroyed, and a huge wave called a tsunami swept onto the shore from the sea.

WHAT'S THE USE OF A ROCK?

Some rocks are hard, some are soft. Some let water through and some do not. Some rocks are smooth, some are very strong, some can be polished to be shiny, and some leave marks. That's why rocks are so useful in so many different ways!

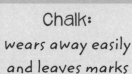

ROCKS

Chalk:
wears away easily and leaves marks

Granite:
hard and impermeable, doesn't wear away

Marble:
can be polished and looks attractive

Slate:
hard and impermeable and splits into thin sheets

Did you know?
Rocks that let water through are called **permeable**.
Rocks that don't let water through are called **impermeable**.

Can you choose the right rock for these jobs?

Tiling a roof

Drawing on a blackboard

Making a statue

Building a castle

FOSSIL SURPRISES

If an animal died and was very quickly buried in mud, sand, or ash, its skeleton could turn into a fossil. But how? Over millions of years, more earth, rocks, and mud ("sediment") would layer on top and press down and eventually turn to rock.

Meanwhile, water passing through the rock slowly dissolves the skeleton bones, but minerals in the water replace the dissolved bone and turn the skeleton into a new kind of rock—a fossil!

Over even more millions of years, the rock around the fossil might wear away so that a bit of the fossil pokes out of the ground. One day somebody might notice it—and that fossil hunter could be you!

Can you help this fossil hunter to find fifteen fossils? First you'll need to help her find the fossil-hunting tools she needs.

Fossil-hunting tools
- Safety glasses
- Geological hammer
- Notebook and pen
- Plastic bag—to put fossil finds in
- Old newspaper—to wrap up delicate finds

15

ROCKY WEATHER

Even though they're big and strong, rocks don't last forever! Rocks that are exposed to the wind and rain slowly get worn away. This is called **weathering** and **erosion**. Water can seep into the rock and soften it so bits fall off more easily, or if the water freezes it can cause a crack to form in the rock. Where there are cracks, plants can start to grow, and their roots can make those cracks even bigger. Wind can carry sand and dust, so when it blows on the rock the blasting slowly wears it away.

When rocks wear away, the landscape can change. These two pictures show a scene before and after the landscape has changed due to weathering and erosion. Can you spot six differences?

SHAPING THE LANDSCAPE

In geological time, weathering causes all sorts of strange and beautiful changes to the landscape. Some of the Earth's most exciting scenery was created over a period of thousands of years.

Weathering

Grand Canyon, USA

Here are some amazing landscapes on Earth today, and a map of where they are found. Can you match them with the pictures of how they looked thousands of years ago when the climate was shaping the landscape? And can you find an explanation for each phenomenon?

Fjords, Norway

Fairy Chimneys, Cappadocia

The Siq, Jordan

Hard basalt rock wears down more slowly than the softer volcanic rock underneath it, leaving mushroom-shaped caps to chimney-like columns.

Glaciers are ice rivers that move slowly down the landscape, carving out valleys as they go.

Rivers erode the landscape, carrying away broken pieces of rock and leaving layers of rock exposed in their path.

The earth pulled apart, leaving a rift in the landscape that was worn smooth by wind and water over thousands of years.

OIL

Oil is very important to our lives: we use it to make medicine, cosmetics, paint, plastics, and fuel. But what has it got to do with rocks? Oil is found deep underground, amongst the rocks, so to get to it, we need to drill big holes in the ground.

How does oil get there?

Millions of years ago, when fish, plants, and tiny sea creatures died, they fell to the bottom of the ocean floor. Their bodies were covered by sediment (sand and mud) and over time, as the layers burying them grew bigger and heavier, they turned to oil, a dark, sticky liquid.

How do we find oil?

Scientists use sound waves to find oil reservoirs. Because sound travels at different speeds through different types of rock, we can send sound waves through the ground and measure how fast they travel—to find the type of rock that holds oil. Then when a likely spot has been found, engineers drill down to see if there is oil where they think it should be.

Help this oil engineer find the best place to drill using the following information. Draw an oil rig on the land in the right place.

- Oil sits on top of porous rock.
- Oil sits underneath impermeable rock.
- Sound waves travel through rock containing oil in this pattern:

  <<<<<<<<<<<

- Your oil rig could look like this:

20

POROUS ROCK

IMPERMEABLE ROCK

GAS

POROUS ROCK

SUPER SOIL

Sitting in layers on top of rock, soil is made from tiny particles of rock mixed with air, water, and bits of dead plants and animals. Soil has different characteristics depending on what kind of rock particles are in it. Soil is what plants grow in—so it is very important to look after it! It develops slowly—but not as slowly as rock.

True or false?
Can you tell which of these soil facts are true? Check your answers on page 32.

Soil can clean water

Soil can be turned into plates and mugs

Soil is home to lots of animals

Soil can be burned as a fuel

Clay soils can be turned into useful things! A lump of clay can be molded and shaped into cups, plates, and bowls—and when baked in a special oven, it keeps its shape and is less likely to break.

Decorate these pottery cups and bowls!

SEE-THROUGH SAND

Some soil contains a lot of sand, which is in fine grains like you see at the beach or in a sand pit. These small parts mean water passes easily through the soil. Sandy soil has a lot of uses:

An ingredient in cement and concrete

An ingredient in bricks

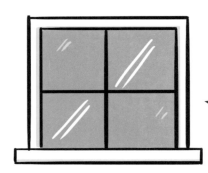

Silica in sand is used to make glass

Growing vegetables

How do you turn soil see-through? By taking the silica from the soil and heating it up with other ingredients you can make glass! If certain other chemicals are added, the glass can be "stained" into colors. You can sometimes see beautiful stained-glass windows in places of worship, like churches and mosques.

Decorate your own stained-glass window here—there's one to color in and one to design yourself. Fill each shape with one color. Will you draw a pattern or a picture?

ROCKS FOR DINNER

Rocks are even important in our kitchens. We need minerals in our diet to keep us healthy—and these minerals are also found in rocks! Even our salt comes from rocks in the earth.

ROCK MENU

IRON:

eggs, lentils, fish, nuts

ZINC:

oysters, spinach, beef, lamb, nuts, dark chocolate

CALCIUM:

milk, kale, yogurt, sardines, cheese

POTASSIUM:

avocado, dried apricot, sweet potato, banana

PHOSPHORUS:

cheese, cola, burgers

MAGNESIUM:

peanuts, whole grain bread, black beans

Use the rock menu to choose a healthy meal that includes at least one of each mineral. Draw your chosen meal on the plates.

THE STONE AGE

Humans who lived around 3.4 million years ago were the first to use rocks and stones as tools. They knew that different stones had different characteristics, making particular rocks better for particular jobs. Here are two stones that we know were very important to Stone Age people:

Flint

A lump of flint can be turned into a sharp tool because—if it is hit carefully with a "hammer" stone—parts of it flake off, leaving sharp, strong edges. It is so strong and sharp that one flake could be made into an arrow that could kill an animal.

Ochre

This rock is red-colored due to the iron in it. When it is ground down into a powder it can be used as paint. One thing people in the Stone Age used this paint for is cave paintings, which have been found all around the world.

These flint axes were found deep in a dark cave. Can you match each axe to its shadow?

Look at the way people and animals are drawn in the cave painting. Using similar colors, draw your own cave painting here.

29

ANSWERS

page 4-5

page 6-7

page 8-9

page 10-11

d	t	h	j	a	e	l	d	k	x	y	d	e	o	h	v	p
y	o	n	u	p	n	t	c	r	i	l	q	g	l	a	v	a
m	p	c	y	i	l	o	v	u	s	e	d	i	n	e	t	a
e	g	s	k	c	r	u	s	t	b	a	k	m	x	i	n	n
t	a	r	o	c	b	i	t	o	d	a	a	a	s	r	t	e
a	n	l	i	g	n	e	o	u	s	t	h	n	i	t	l	l
m	f	z	y	j	l	t	t	j	s	v	e	t	l	u	e	a
o	y	m	g	o	e	u	n	c	t	d	p	l	m	a	u	i
r	c	v	x	s	g	j	e	r	n	i	n	e	v	u	d	l
p	r	s	r	i	f	p	e	n	l	o	v	u	h	d	o	p
h	e	t	u	m	c	v	i	o	g	l	r	u	f	c	e	a
i	h	n	h	a	i	e	i	n	n	y	d	r	x	a	n	m
c	t	j	u	r	b	c	k	s	t	i	m	n	o	t	l	u
d	s	y	i	s	y	f	d	t	z	h	a	a	m	o	u	r
s	y	v	v	o	l	c	u	j	a	m	g	o	s	e	y	c
s	e	d	i	m	e	n	t	a	r	y	m	c	r	i	y	j
m	e	r	c	u	r	y	s	e	o	j	a	v	t	f	v	a

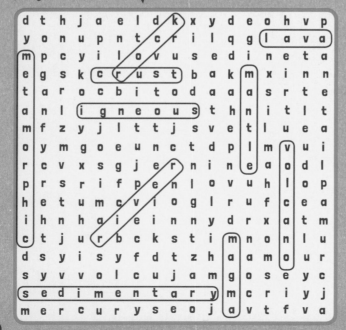

Tiling a roof

- SLATE

Drawing on a blackboard

- CHALK

Making a statue

- MARBLE

Building a castle

- GRANITE

page 16-17

page 18-19

Rivers erode the landscape, carrying away broken pieces of rock and leaving layers of rock exposed in their path.

Glaciers are ice rivers that move slowly down the landscape, carving out valleys as they go.

The earth pulled apart, leaving a rift in the landscape that was worn smooth by wind and water over thousands of years.

Hard basalt rock wears down more slowly than the softer volcanic rock underneath it, leaving mushroom-shaped caps to chimney-like columns.

Page 20-21

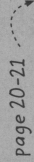 

OIL AREA

page 22

Trick question!
-
They are all **TRUE!**

page 28-29

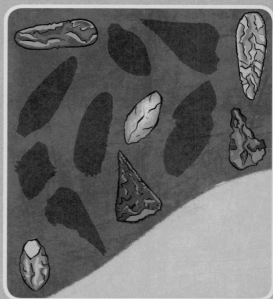